Andrea L. Hines

I0617985

AND IT IS SO

Volume 1
A Collection of the Best of 8@8

Studio Griffin
A Publishing Company
www.studiogriffin.net

For information, contact:
Studio Griffin
A Publishing Company
studiogriffin@outlook.com
www.studiogriffin.net

Cover Design by Ruth E. Griffin
Image by © Mark Baldwin / Adobe

First Edition

ISBN-13: 978-1-954818-42-2

Library of Congress Control Number: 2023935852

1 2 3 4 5 6 7 8 9 10

On Monday, Wednesday, and Friday of each week, ALH Broadcasting programs of inspiration, encouragement, and thanksgiving air on a variety of platforms for internet radio / TV, including FB, YouTube and SIBN.net.

At 8:00am, for 8 minutes, people tune in to receive a Victory Verse and a Positive Point of Power to guide their day. At 8:00pm we tune in again to give God praise and thanksgiving for who He is and all He has done. The programs have been fondly titled 8@8!

This first volume is dedicated to the morning crew and the night shift of 8@8. I could not have done this without their commitment and faithfulness to go with me on this journey to grow in God. I pray these excerpts will continue to strengthen and encourage all of us for generations to come.

A GOOD AND GRACIOUS GOD

I woke up this morning
with Jesus on my mind.
Before I even began to pray,
I thought about the time
He provided and protected,
kept me from hurt and harm.
When I was at my lowest,
He just wrapped me in His arms.
He gave me peace and comfort,
pulled me from the storm I was in.
And even now if I slip, then repent,
He still forgives my sin.
I thought of the cross,
the pain He endured,
I thought of His love for me,
how He sacrificed,
how He paid the price that day on Calvary.
He's been whatever I've needed Him to be,
no matter what I've done or where.
He always has a way of letting me know
I'm not alone – He's there.
There's so much I could share with you
about His goodness and His grace.
All the times He's healed
every bruised and broken place.
But I know I just can't tell it all
and neither can any of you.

We each have our own testimony
of what just the name Jesus can do
Spend time with Him today –
in worship, intentional and pure.
Spend time with Him today
in gratitude make your calling and election sure.
Spend time with Him and give Him
the praise, and the glory, and the honor He's due
I know I can't make it without Him
and if truth be told, neither can you.

Positive Point Of Power
He Did It For Me

I am sometimes overwhelmed at how much God loves me, in spite of the things I did before I understood who He is. He never left me in spite of me. Even when I didn't give him the honor He deserves, he never ever turned away from me. Now that I have a relationship with Him, I will not let a day go by without acknowledging his love, power, and presence in my life and all He's done for me.

A REMINDER

Lord, when I've needed some direction,
not knowing what to do,
that's the time I'd lift my hands
in total praise to You.
When I thought, "I can't go on –
my strength I must renew,"
that's when I'd stop and sing
a song of worship just for You.
At times when I felt all alone
for friends were very few,
that's when I was reminded
that my greatest friend is You.
Even faced with struggle
you allowed me to go through,
I knew that I could make it
just as long as I had you.
In every situation whenever I would call
You'd show up and You'd show out –
able to shift it all.
If you find yourself in circumstances
like this through the week,
remember things can turn around
if God is whom you seek.
You don't have to live in doubt, or even in defeat,
take it to the Lord and leave it at His feet.
Be encouraged, you have help,
God is never far away.
He wants you to call on Him
so He can guide your way.

These are just reminders
of what the Lord will do
when you remember who He is
and what He's done for you.

Positive Point Of Power
I Have Help

One of the most important facets of my existence is to know I am not alone. The help I have is supernatural, omnipotent, omnipresent, and omniscient. Jesus is my help, and He is well able. I don't have to be concerned with the adversary of how. How am I going to make it? How am I going to do it? How am I going to get it? How? Easy! I have help. I don't have to stay stuck, or struggle, or stress. My help has me covered and all is well.

ABUNDANTLY BLESSED

You are so blessed, abundantly blessed
and God's not finished yet,
though the enemy wants you to spend your time
at the wishing well of regret.
"I wish I had a better job, a finer car or house.
I wish I had more money in the bank,
or perhaps a more loving spouse."
Don't stay focused on what you don't have
in material, tangible stuff.
Get a flashback of what God's brought you through
and that should be enough
to send you into perpetual praise
for where you are right now.
Things may not be perfect, but they're better anyhow
because you're blessed.
After all, you're still alive to greet another day.
You're blessed because a sovereign God's
still there to lead the way.
Your circumstance may be challenging,
your situation may not be the best,
but no matter where you are today,
you are still abundantly blessed.
You serve a God who loves you
and hears your every cry.
He works things together for your good.
He's not a man that He should lie.
You have His favor, His grace,

His mercy, His joy to keep you strong --
His peace, and don't forget the faith
you can activate all day long.
Yes, you are blessed, abundantly blessed.
Therefore, you have no choice
other than to bless His Holy name
and rejoice... rejoice... rejoice!!

Positive Point Of Power
Blessed And Highly Favored

Regardless of what I have, what I may be missing, what I think I need, I reflect on Paul's words in Philippians 4:11-12...

> "I have learned in whatever situation I am in to be content. I know how to be abased, and I know how to abound. Everywhere and in all things, I have learned both to be full and to be hungry both to abound and to suffer need."

...because I know I am abundantly blessed!

ACCEPTING MY ASSIGNMENT

When I woke up this morning,
I had a smile upon my face.
I was aware of God's new mercies
and His amazing grace.
I thought about His love
and how His Son had died for me.
I thought about the blood that Jesus shed on Calvary.
I know I have no time to waste, no time to complain.
Since God has renewed my mind,
I must not stay the same.
I must be Kingdom-minded,
worldly things I will not hold.
I must decrease and die to self, and let God take control.
I must embrace the fact that when I woke up today
a sovereign God already knew
what He'd have me do and say.
That's why it's so important to let Him direct my way.
He has the divine download with the details for my day.
There's an assignment for me that only I can do.
It is as unique to me as your assignment is to you.
I trust the Lord, though I admit I may not understand,
I still trust the process, and the pathway and the plan.
Father, I know there's purpose
in whatever I put my hands to do,
and I know I want to do the things
that bring glory to You
Because I am your handiwork and I am your creation.

There's no need for me
to lean on my inept interpretation.
So, guide me, oh great Jehovah,
I'll follow where you lead.
I'm equipped and I'm submitted.
I have everything I need
to accomplish the assignment
that You have for me today.
I'll adhere to your instructions Lord,
just show me the way.

Positive Point Of Power
Ready Willing And Able

After I completed the victory verse and God had given me the positive point of power, He did something unusual. He added the following lines:

"You've been bought with a price, you are not your own, you're here for a reason and you are not alone."

They seemed like an afterthought, but I have learned that everything with God is intentional, so I was obedient. I read them after I had shared everything else. Someone commented, "I needed those extra lines."

To God be the glory, I am so grateful for the unction of the Holy Spirit to do everything just the way God said.

BE OF GOOD COURAGE

Do you ever wake up wondering
if you'll ever make it through?
You may be feeling overwhelmed
by whatever you have to do.
You may be struggling in this season.
You may be dealing with delay.
It really doesn't matter
what you're facing day to day,
when you remember that His timing
always shows his sovereignty.
You have that bold assurance
that you have the victory.
Don't start your day complaining
or having a double mind.
Just know that God's all-knowing
and He'll step in right on time.
God always has a process
in preparation for His plan
to come into fruition
while He holds you in His hand.
He's always up to something.
Believe for your breakthrough.
Don't quit. Know that you qualify
for what He has for you.
Stand and trust the Father,
let every word you speak
be a declaration of His promises.

Be of good courage, don't retreat.
And every time you praise the Lord,
in good times, or in bad,
you'll discover more of His peace and power
than you have ever had.
Thank You Jesus! Hallelujah!
From mountain top to valley wide
you can rejoice knowing all is well,
for God is on your side!!

Positive Point Of Power
I'm More Than A Conqueror

We all have those moments when you are tested to stand on what you believe about God. He has shown His goodness, His grace and the fact that He can do anything but fail. But when times are uncertain, that's when we have to remember, having done all, stand. Stand in the whole armor of God without fear, without doubt, and without wavering.

Psalm 27:14 in the Message Bible says it best, "Stay with God! Take heart. Don't quit."

I'll say it again: "Stay with God."

Be of good courage.

BEGIN WITH GOD

So many times, we say there are things
we really want to do,
yet we fail to have the discipline we need
to see them through.
That discipline begins
before we get into our day.
It starts as soon as we wake up
and take time out to pray.
Since we have a brand-new start,
we can make a choice
to begin each day with You, Lord God,
and listen for your voice.
If we never fail to seek You first
(and I mean without delay)
we'll stay on track, we won't fall back,
and we won't lose our way.
The more time that we spend with You,
the less likely we'll be
to move away from purpose
and then miss our destiny.
Each day, we are determined
to get Your clear directions
and focus on what pleases You
and not our imperfections.
We'll hold on to Your Word, dear Lord,
no matter what we face
and let Your love and joy flow freely
while you show us grace.
Regardless of what lies ahead,

or what we have to do
we vow that we'll be disciplined
to begin each day with You.

Positive Point Of Power
GOD FIRST

It takes discipline to form habits that make up our daily routine—our regimen, if you will. Certain things we do in the morning especially and then things that occupy our evening before we go to bed. It's paramount that we set the tone for the day in order to be productive and move towards our purpose. While there will always be things that are out of our control, we can't let the day just 'happen.' We need to begin with the power and authority God has given us. The best way to do that is to seek Him first. Put Him at the top of your agenda and everything else will fall into place.

BUILT IN BACK UP

Whatever struggles are before you,
whatever decisions you have to make –
you might be fighting an addiction
or some habit you have to break –
you are not in it by yourself.
God is greater than
and when you really believe that,
you'll be able to stand.
Everyone has issues
and they can take on any form.
They're designed to take you down,
but that's not meant to be your norm.
Issues want you fearful,
but God didn't give fear to you.
You may not see your victory,
but God will see you through
He is always with you,
whatever challenges you face
You don't have to cower in a corner.
He is your hiding place.
Remember Christ in you the hope of glory,
whatever you need to see you through
you have a God, He's well able,
and He's living inside of you.

Positive Point Of Power
I Have Built In Back Up

Issues, struggles, trials, storms, tests—we will all have them or face them from time to time. You may reach out for help only to discover it can't be found, at least not from man. How wonderful it is to know help is already with you, it's already in you, because God is always there.

BUMPS IN THE ROAD

Just when you think you've got it made,
it never ever fails,
life will throw a punch
that knocks the wind out of your sails.
You may think all is going well
and things are silky smooth.
You've finally hit your rhythm
and you're right there in the groove.
Then before you know it, something unforeseen
will rock you to your knees,
threatening to shatter every dream.
Sometimes you do the best you can,
yet even when you do
it never seems enough…
the world will still want more from you.
When you face discouragement,
disappointment, or pain,
you can't shut down.
God's whispering,
"Get up and try again,"
God says, *"Don't shut down, hold on …*
I know just where you are.
I know what you are going through.
I'm never very far.
Everything that happens, I am in the midst.
You were meant for purpose, not to just exist.
These are simply bumps in the road.
You will pass them by.
You cannot avoid them, so don't you even try.

Though you didn't see it coming,
or thought it would never be,
don't panic, know I'm in control,
and then draw close to me.
You may not fully understand
the way I'll have you take
just know that life might make you bend,
but you will never break."

Positive Point Of Power
I Am Unbreakable

The good thing I've discovered about bumps in the road is whether they appear unexpectedly or have a warning sign that lets you know you can expect them ahead; just they can only slow you down. They aren't designed to stop you. They aren't there to create permanent redirection and make you feel your journey has come to an end. They simply remind you a momentary change of pace is sometimes all you need.

CHANGE

Sometimes in my 'desire to do,'
I have to take a pause
and remember I'm not perfect,
I still have faults and flaws.
All of us at times have pointed our finger
at someone and highlighted their shortcomings,
as if we didn't have a single one.
There may be things in us
we don't want anyone to see.
Could this be time for transformation
and increased 'knee-ology?"
Take it to the Lord in prayer,
confess to Him if no one else.
He already knows your struggles
as you try to daily die to self.
In my quiet time of introspection,
and when I take time to pray
I'm humbled and I'm grateful
and this is what I say...

Father, I don't have it all together, wish I could say I do,
but there are things I know I need that only come from You.
Thank You for your provision and Your divine protection.
I also need your guidance and with that, divine correction.
I know that there are things I need to work on every day.
You are still the potter, and I am still the clay.
I surrender all as You hold me in your hands.
Have your way in my life today,
I'm submitted to Your plans.
Mold me and shape me Father,

into what I need to be
so those that I encounter
only see the Christ in me.
Let me show someone empathy;
let me show Your grace and glory;
and not be quick to judge someone
when I don't know their story.
Father, continue to work on me
and let me not forget
You are God and God alone
and it's not over for me yet.

Positive Point Of Power
Let There Be A Change In Me

In times of introspection and reflection, I must look in the mirror for change before I look anywhere else. We all have imperfections and thank goodness God continues to work on each one of us. I am my own assignment. It is not for me to judge anyone else. My responsibility is to go before my Father and allow Him to change me so that I am equipped and enabled for the work of the Kingdom.

CONNECTIVITY

I wanted to pull from a victory verse
already penned in rhythm and rhyme
but I couldn't find the right words and flow,
at least not at first this time.
I had heard four words earlier this week
that I know came from Him.
God has His way of doing things,
so I waited to yield my pen
and do what I felt He wanted me to do
and write what He wanted me to say.
He always knows what we need and when,
because He's guiding us each day
So I had to sit and wait a bit,
but this is what I heard Him say…
"Tell them
STAY CONNECTED TO CHRIST
no matter what the situation
I know this isn't brand new
or some grand deep revelation,
but rather a reminder
of where your help comes from.
You have power
that's only given through Jesus Christ, the Son
of God who has all the answers.
He's the door, the vine, the way;
seek ye first the Kingdom, listen when you pray.
When test and trials confront you,
especially the unexpected,
don't scratch your head, and scurry and worry,

He said,
"Just stay connected."
I'm going to stop writing now,
I don't want to get into me.
Stay Connected to Christ,
He'll show you exactly what you need to see.

Positive Point Of Power
Stay Connected To Christ

There is a continuing thread when it comes to Christ and our relationship with Him. He is our source, and He wants us to spend time with Him. He wants us to seek Him, hear His voice and be obedient to His will and His way. As for me, when I stay connected to Him nothing can stop me because nothing can stop the plans of God and I am part of the plan!

DAILY STRATEGY

Every day is precious, that should be our attitude.
The first words that we speak each day
should be words of gratitude.
We don't know all the day will hold,
but we know who holds the day,
a mighty God whose face we seek
so that He can direct our way.
Life brings daily challenges
that each of us must face,
that's why God's mercies
are new every morning
and why He grants us grace.
To navigate those rough times
and do the best we can,
for everything is purposeful
and all part of His plan.
At times the challenges seem huge;
other times they are so small
and we handle them so well,
they don't seem like challenges at all.
Either way, when our lifestyles include
worship, praise and prayer;
when we expect the unexpected
and always know that God's still there,
the road gets a little easier,
the days a little brighter
and whatever burden is weighing us down
will get a little lighter.
Your challenge and how you handle it
is unique to you

That's why we tend to avoid the phrase,
"I know what you're going through."
There's strength found in the struggle
whatever it may be.
There's power in the testimony
you will share with me.
There's provision God will send
when and where you least expect it
so when someone wants to bless you,
receive it, don't reject it.

Positive Point Of Power
Seize The Day

When I open my eyes, I am ecstatic because God has granted me another day. Another day to be used for His glory. Another day to see Him move for me, with me, and through me. Another day to marvel at His miraculous power. Another day to experience His goodness, His grace, and His mercy. Another day to feel His love surround me as I thank Him for all He's done just because I am His own.

DELAYS

Delays: perceived as something bad
will interrupt your day.
They upset your agenda,
could put roadblocks in your way.
Might be a simple traffic stall,
a detour you didn't foresee,
a ride that was late, a forgotten date
so many things it could be
to hold you up or slow you down,
either could be the case.
It doesn't seem fair, with no time to spare
you must now re-set your pace.
Don't let yourself get frustrated
or throw a childish fit.
Breathe and use the time
to give God praise in all of it.
Delays may divert hurt or harm,
keep danger from your door.
Just redirect your energy
and praise God all the more.
Whenever there's postponement,
Satan things he has a chance
to initiate confusion,
so praise God in advance.
Wake up each day
thankful for what He's already done.
Keep a praise upon your lips
for what is about to come
is all part of His awesome plan,

His grand design for you.
Each delay is just God's way
of divinely preparing you
for blessings He wants you to have.
Don't worry, embrace delays.
Know they have a purpose.
Trust God and give Him praise.

Positive Point Of Power
Embrace Delays With A Praise

The day I came to realize delays are like seeing the glass half full is the day I truly understood the reason for giving thanks IN everything. Whatever God does, and whenever He chooses to do it, it's for my good and for His glory. For this He is deserving of a premeditated praise on purpose.

DIRECTION

Let the morning bring news
of your unfailing love
each day throughout the week.
I lean not to my own understanding,
Lord, instead Your face I seek.
I will strive to be a blessing,
in all the things I do.
My aim is to complete my tasks
in a way that is pleasing to You.
Give me the tongue of the learned, Oh Lord
that I might know how to speak
a word to encourage the weary and
add strength to one who is weak.
Cause me to hear You whisper to me as
Your faithfulness sees me through.
Because of Your love,
I am not consumed.
Each morning your mercies are new.
I open my eyes and I'm grateful.
I prepare to continue this race
and tell someone the good news
about God's saving grace.
Thank You Lord for Your goodness,
for letting me see a new day.
I entrust my life to you and say,
"Father, please show me the way."

Positive Point Of Power
Divine Direction Is Key For Me

There is something about His presence in the morning that establishes a positive pattern for my day. As long as I have divine direction, I will continue on the path that leads me to my purpose. I no longer have to worry, I can worship. I don't have to stress because I am strengthened whenever I seek His face. Gratitude and grace are the perfect combination for the manifestation of His promises, and I will do His will His way.

DON'T BLOCK YOUR BREAKTHROUGH

Most of us are believing God
for something, great or small.
We sincerely seek the Father
because He sees and knows it all.
But there are times we think
His promises may not manifest
because the enemy is at work
trying to block us from God's best.
All he has is his suggestions.
Don't waste your precious time.
The devil is a liar.
You keep Jesus on your mind.
Be confident in knowing
that the Word of God is true
and because a Sovereign God has said it,
guess what, so should you.
Just because things haven't happened
when you thought they should
trust the process, let God work it all
together for your good.
Stop entertaining doubt and then speaking unbelief.
These things delay your destiny
and the breakthrough that you seek
Don't waver in this season,
stand, stay ready to receive
and let your countenance and conversation
show that you believe.

Positive Point Of Power
Speak The Word

I have discovered if I lean to my own understanding I will inevitably get in my own way. All of us have the innate ability to self-sabotage and that's what the enemy is counting on happening. That doesn't have to be the case. Don't doubt and delay your destiny. Don't waver in unbelief and veer from your path prematurely, which will cause you to falter in your timing rather than flourish in His. Believe God and speak His word.

Period.

That's it... that's all... and that's good enough for me.

EXPECTATION

I set my day in motion
just as blessed as I can be.
You see I am God's handiwork
and He has plans for me.
He has plans for me to prosper,
plans for me to be in health,
good things are not withheld…
He gives me power to get wealth.
Whatever the enemy stole from me
to shake me to my core
I'm taking back, and besides that,
God will give me more.
I woke up, more than a conqueror.
I woke up with victory.
I know that I abide in God,
and He abides in me.
I will linger in His presence
when I take time to pray
and yield to the direction
that He downloads for my day.
I don't know how your day began,
or what you're going through.
But I can tell you God is faithful
and He will take care of you.
If He said it, He will do it.
He can't fail and He can't lie.
He can change your situation
in the twinkling of an eye.
Keep your faith and hope in God

and you will be amazed
Give Him all the glory,
worship Him and give Him praise.

Positive Point Of Power
Expect His Best

God, I thank You for every day You have made and allow me to enjoy. My expectation is high, fueled by the realization You want to give me Your best and Your promises shall come to pass. Because You are the same yesterday, today, and forever I am confident that you will do exactly what You said. Father, you are my everything and my heart is filled with gratitude for You are forever faithful. Amen and Amen.

FEAR IS DEFEATED

You're feeling stuck. You don't know why...
can't seem to move ahead.
Something may have happened,
or words may have been said,
but a seed was planted
that caused your heart to race a bit.
Fear was knocking
at your dreams and plans
and now you want to quit.
And when that door was opened
and fear had entrance in,
suddenly you found that doubt
became your new best friend.
Before you knew it, there you were,
stopped dead in your tracks.
You could not take one step forward
as fear kept you looking back.
God said to remind you,
"What fear would have you see
is deception to distract you
and keep your mind off Me."
Stay focused on the Word of God.
He's still in control.
Speak in the name of Jesus
and fear must release its hold.
You know the enemy's defeated
and there's nothing fear can do
Weapons formed will never prosper.
God's still right there with you.

Guard your heart and guard your mind
from things you see and hear
Just remember, God is with you,
so you have no need to fear.

Positive Point Of Power
There's No Fear Here

God has not given you a spirit of fear but of power, love, and a sound mind. Fear is a trick of the enemy to put you in a place where you become paralyzed to move forward because doubt has become your constant companion. Doubt is a distraction that will ultimately create a pathway to your demise. Rest assured you have power over a defeated devil, so fear is not part of your future.

FOLLOWING INSTRUCTIONS

Because You've given me instructions
to give thanks IN everything
I will be sure to give You praise
no matter what life brings.
I will praise You in the sunshine
and even in the rain.
I will praise You when my heart aches
and in the throes of pain.
It might be easier to praise You
when I'm not in a fight.
It might be easier to thank You
when things are going right.
But no matter what it looks like
or what I'm going through,
I'll stand on every Word You said
and give all praise to You.
Even when doubt, defeat, and fear
attempt to enter in,
I'll clap my hands and give You praise
over, and over again.
Lord, You've been so faithful.
You've shown so much love for me.
I know everything I am, or ever hope to be
is all because you cared so much.
You wrapped me up in You.
You cannot lie or fail
and You do what you intended to.

With gratitude, I'll heed Your Word
whatever You require.
I just want to do Your will,
that's my greatest desire.
IN everything I'll give You thanks
just like You said I should,
because I know You'll work all things
together for my good.

Positive Point Of Power
Raise A Perpetual Praise

God never stops. He never gets tired, and His day never
ends. What's more He never ever fails. Regardless of
what I do He holds me close and asks very little in
return. To give Him thanks IN everything is an
instruction I have no difficulty following because He's
always up to something that will bless me beyond
measure.

FORGIVE FOR REAL

There's no one who can go through life
without some type of pain
or injustice that's so great
you feel you'll never be the same.
Maybe someone hurt you,
maybe someone 'did you wrong.'
The question is, just how long
will you sing the victim song?
If you really want to stop the pain
and turn your life around;
if you really want to be set free
so you're no longer bound,
don't rehearse the hurt you feel.
You have to let it go.
If you don't, that root of bitterness
will grow, and grow, and grow
and choke the life right out of you,
the life you want to live.
You won't be able to receive.
You won't know how to give.
You won't be able to enjoy
the things God has in store
You'll be too busy holding on to things
you should ignore.
Ignore means you can 'disregard,'
and 'take no notice of.'
It also means you have matured
and handled things with love.
When love is activated, that's when you finally know

you can forgive and when you do,
you can let things go.
Take note: you can't forgive a thing,
then say you can't forget.
Real forgiveness is for you and is without regret.
Don't harbor unforgiveness, or let anger take control,
or think you can't get past the pain
that may have taken hold.
When you give it all to God and love as He loves you,
forgive and forget is not rhetoric,
it's truly what you do.
Take back your joy, take back your peace.
Now you know the way
to really be completely free,
forgive someone today!

Positive Point Of Power
Forgive For Real

Forgiveness is the first step on the path to becoming healed and whole. The second step is forgetting. They are both encapsulated in your power to choose.

Choose wisely.

GOD OMNIPOTENT

New dawn, new day...
I'm determined to do the best I can
to represent the Kingdom well
and follow the Master's plan.
I greet the day excited
because I know whatever I missed
God can orchestrate a turnaround –
so I must resist
the urge to concentrate on yesterday's mistakes.
They can't govern my today.
I have His mercy and His grace.
The word says for me to give attention
to what God's doing right now
and not to get all worked up about tomorrow anyhow.
I feel strong, nothing can stop me.
I have God on my side.
I am chosen... I am called... and I cannot be denied.
If God told me it's my season,
and He said that it's my time,
if He promised me His blessings,
then I know that they are mine.
When I give my testimony, anytime I share my story
I will talk about His goodness and give Him all the glory.
I remember who He is and all He's done for me.
I am perfectly positioned to be what He wants me to be.
When I say, "This is the day the Lord has made, I'll
rejoice and be glad,"
it's because for me, it could very well be,
the best day I've ever had.

And here's the really good news,
because He loves you too,
whatever good things He's done for me,
He'll do the same for you.
Let the joy of the Lord be your strength today
and let gratitude prevail.
Remember you serve a mighty God
who cannot lie and cannot fail.
Lift your eyes to the hills, praise Him in advance,
even if you falter, He'll give you another chance.
Today be encouraged, think of what the Lord can do.
there's nothing too hard for a mighty God,
so there's nothing too hard for you.

Positive Point Of Power
Remember Who He Is

To serve an omnipotent God who has chosen me for a specific work sometimes leaves me speechless. How can I possibly articulate His power, His presence, and His love towards me. I will gladly present my body as a living sacrifice. It is my reasonable service to a God who knows who I am and loves me still. In my imperfection I am blessed by a perfect God and I will not forget.

HE PLACED IT IN ME

Whenever you look at things in the natural,
there may not be much to see,
but I'm not governed by what it looks like,
rather what God's promised me.
You might look at my situation
and think I'm barely getting by,
However, God can change my circumstances
in the twinkling of an eye.
I will not speak from a pitiful place
of always being in need.
I will not confess what I do not have
or plant a 'poor me' seed.
By the way, I'm not a borrower.
God said that I would lend.
If I want from time to time,
that's a temporary state I'm in.
God has plans for me to prosper,
plans for me to be in health,
plans for me to be a blessing.
I've been designed for wealth.
There's power in my words
and at the mention of His name,
everything can shift so lack won't be my claim to fame
I am blessed and highly favored,
abundance is my story.
God supplies my every need
according to His riches in glory.
I know exactly who I am and who my Father is.
I carry Kingdom DNA and that's because I'm His.

Now I might require
some adjustment, some alignment and correction,
but I'm a tither and a giver with a covenant connection.
And God will bless what's in my hands,
rebuke the devourer too.
One thing I know for certain,
He will do what He said He will do
I am the righteousness of God,
greater is He that is in me.
Don't be fooled by the outward appearance,
wait, and see the victory!

Positive Point Of Power
I Have What I Need

I am an excellent example of the plan of God. He has given me all I will ever need to be what He designed me to be and have what He intends for me to have. I may not see it all today in the natural but in the spirit, it has already come to pass. That's why an advanced praise is always in order. I am fashioned for the phenomenal and God makes no mistakes.

JUST FOR ME

You can speak with wisdom
where others are concerned.
You can tell your testimony
and the lessons you have learned.
You can believe in faith with others,
connect with them in prayer,
tell them when they stand in need,
"Trust God. He's always there."
People come to you for everything,
their perception is you're strong.
Yet there are times
(if truth be told), they couldn't be more wrong.
While you can give encouragement,
and you often do,
if you're not careful, you'll be void
when it comes to encouraging you.
Unless you take time out for yourself,
you'll have no strength to stand.
God expects you to find balance
to continue with His plan.
Sometimes you need refreshing; time to just kick back,
time to be still, or refuel and refill,
time to regroup and just relax.
It's not that you're trying to hide and
you don't want to appear to be rude,
and you are not developing a self-centered attitude.
But in order for you to stay on track there are things
you must address,
that have nothing to do with anyone else.

Sometimes you just need the rest.

Positive Point Of Power
Time Out – Preapproved

To be able to be present for other people and be the blessing you want to be, you could find yourself out of balance, out of time, and out of strength. It is not God's intent for you to give all you have until you are sometimes wanting to give up, give in or give out. That is not His will for you. Only when you rest can you refuel with the resolve to see things through.

MOOD AND ATTITUDE

Bored? Tired? Nothing to do?
Feel like your days never end?
At times down and defeated?
Discouraged before you begin?
Same old same old, over and over,
wish there was something new?
Here's a little food for thought
that could make a difference for you.
Change your mood and your attitude.
I know it sounds cliché
but I can pretty much guarantee
it will shift things in your day.
You may not think you're complaining,
or showing ingratitude,
but whining about your circumstance
puts you in a negative mood.
If you took your mind off of yourself
and made an effort instead,
to concentrate on ways to bless someone else,
you'd surely come out ahead.
Your attitude will begin to change,
joy will start filling your heart.
With every unselfish act you complete,
it's as if you make a fresh start.
There's more to life
than your circumstance or your current situation.
Give of yourself through a kind word or deed

and do it without hesitation.
Let God's love flow freely from you.
Let it so govern your mood
that before you know it
a positive vibe will take over your attitude.
Mark this day as a turnaround
to do whatever you can
to let your mood and your attitude
uplift your fellow man.
And while you're at it, you'll be surprised
at what else this change will do.
Whenever you show the light and love of Christ,
it will also uplift you.

Positive Point Of Power
Check Yourself

It's very easy to play the blame game when you're not at your best. It must be due to something someone did or said that put in the mindset of the glass half empty. The last thing you want is a time of self-examination but that's the first thing you need. Take a look at you, a really good look. If you continue to experience the same 'downers,' chances are you are the common denominator and a change in you is the change you need.

MY HUMBLE PRAYER

In moments of uncertainty,
when I'm unsure of what to do,
Father, I know I need a moment
for some quiet time with you,
When I want to please You, Lord,
and do the things I think I should,
Let me separate the 'God' ideas
from those that are simply 'good.'
If I'm unsure if my present path
is the one You are commanding,
I'll put on Your armor, Lord,
and that will keep me standing.
Bridle my tongue please, Father.
Let me be careful of what I say.
Let no corrupt communication
pass through my lips today.
And just in case I'm tempted to doubt
or even fear,
let my faith be activated
since You're God and You're right here.
Thank You for hearing my every prayer
'cause when I'm going through,
regardless of the time of day,
I can always talk to you.
Father, your grace and mercy
let me know I'm truly blessed,
But in the stillness of this moment,
I have one more request.
Because I know You love me

and You've set me apart,
When I pray, and I give way,
I ask You,
Lord, speak to my heart!

Positive Point Of Power
Let The Lord Speak

The times I feel the presence of God so strongly that tears flow down my face freely and uncontrollably, I can hardly contain myself as I wait for Him to speak to me as only He can. A moment with Him can be written on my heart and etched in my memory forever.

POSITION IT IN PRAYER

We know that we're God's chosen.
We know we love His Word.
At times, we want to act
upon the things we've seen and heard.
We want to rescue everyone; do all we know to do.
But God's designed a process
that He takes each of us through.
You may be anointed,
and all that's well and good.
Some things are 'Jesus Only' –
turn them over as you should.
When you're given information,
someone feels they just must share,
you've really been informed
so you'll position it in prayer.
Take it to the Father.
Everything is not for you
to act upon, and in the flesh,
see what you can do.
We're called to love our neighbor
and God wants us to care.
Since He holds the master plan,
position things in prayer.
And please don't pray the problem,
that will just make matters worse.
Remember: words released can be a blessing or a curse.
No matter what the circumstance,

or burden brought to bear,
know a sovereign God's still in control.
position everything in prayer!

Positive Point Of Power
Prayer Is Part Of The Process

I am obligated to talk to the Father and prayer is my opportunity to dialog with Him. There is no better way to minister to the Lord; no better way to give Him glory; no better way to receive His instruction than in prayer.

No better way...

POWER UP

Here's something I've come to know for sure,
when all is said and done,
whatever fight I'm facing, I've already won.
Whether sickness in my body,
or an assignment that I dread
I won't dare complain.
I will raise a praise instead!
If I get discouraged sometimes along the way
and I need to power up, this is what I say:
I'm more than a conqueror and I am not my own.
I serve a mighty faithful God and I am not alone.
I have power, I have purpose; man can't do one thing to me.
No weapon formed will prosper. If you believe you'll see,
as long as I have Jesus I need not be concerned.
I'll just search the scriptures, and every Word I've learned
I will speak into the atmosphere and watch it come to pass.
I will walk in love as Christ and not become as sounding brass.
I won't faint. I won't fall. I will be merciful to all
just as God His been to me.
Because of Him I've been made free.
He gives me words that give me strength –
part of my affirmation –
and I give Him all the glory as His one-of-a-kind creation.
So wherever you are in your day today,
let me say to you:
power up and keep the faith.
He'll always see you through!

Positive Point Of Power
Tap In And Power Up

God is so good that He placed in me all I would ever need in order to accomplish His will for me in the earth. Then He gave me free will and the ability to choose. As I acknowledge Him and He orders my steps, I recognize the power within and activate my authority as His child.

Oh, what a mighty God I serve!

PRESS ON

Sometimes you'll find
that there are things that simply disturb your peace.
Be it person, place, or thing,
you want the irritant to cease.
Seems like whenever you get focused
on time with God and prayer,
there's something that distracts you
that you didn't realize was there.
You may not have seen it yesterday, or the day before.
Right now, it's vexing you
and you don't want to deal with it anymore.
Subconsciously you ignored it,
at least you thought you had,
but for whatever reason 'it' has raised its head again.
It's like the thorn Paul talked about –
God remove this thorn from me,
yet the thorn was necessary
for what God wanted Paul to see.
He wanted Paul to know that His grace was enough
and Paul need not be bothered
by all the other worrisome stuff.
There may be limitations
and sometimes things may look bleak.
Don't you know God will renew your strength
whenever you are weak.
This is when you must remember
the things that God has said,
and there is so much good
that you will find around the bend ... just up ahead.

If you don't embrace distractions
and give them permission to grow,
and refocus your attention
on the Word of God you know,
and keep moving, you'll be strengthened,
equipped for what God wants you to do.
There's something on the other side,
if you'll keep pressing and see things through.

Positive Point Of Power
Push Past It

Regardless of what it looks like, or how difficult it may be, if it's part of God's plan, it is purposeful. If it's purposeful, I need to do it. If I need to do it, He's equipped me for it. If He's equipped me for it, I already have victory over it. I have to push. I cannot quit. I have come too far, and I will not be denied.

PRIVATE TIME

Father, thank you for another day...
as I open up my eyes.
No matter what I have to do –
no matter how time flies
each moment with You is precious.
Each moment with You has meaning.
The more time that I spend with You,
the less time I spend leaning
to my own understanding.
I'll put faith-filled trust in You
to guide me and direct my path,
doing all You said You would do.
You are an awesome God,
you always have the time.
I remember scripture clearly says,
"Seek and you will find."
So I continued to seek His face
and settled myself to hear
and as soon as I felt His presence,
He whispered in my ear...
"The enemy wants to keep us apart
because He knows My plan.
Stay focused. Continue to seek My face
before you seek My hand.
Let me orchestrate your day and tell you what to do.
Don't be anxious or distracted. Let me prioritize for you."
Thank You, Heavenly Father, for ordering my day.
Orchestrate my every move,
Lord, show me the way

and even if I get off track
and I don't get it right,
thank You for a second
to do what's pleasing in Your sight.
Thank you, Lord, for loving me
and giving me time to pray.
I look forward to every moment
that I will spend with you today.

Positive Point Of Power
Nothing Shall Separate Me

When I spend time with the Father I enter into a space where nothing is as important as His presence and our time together. It's a place that I don't want to leave; and when I do, I can't wait to return.

Father, take me there again...

READY

I am the righteousness of God
and I am ready for the day.
I am clothed in His armor,
equipped for whatever comes my way.
I've spent some time in worship,
I've taken time to pray,
I've waited patiently to hear what Jesus had to say.
He is a sovereign God and I know the path's been set
for me to do His Will His way without a single regret.
I may not understand all things,
but I'm of the persuasion
fear plus doubt can never be part of my life's equation.
Faith plus obedience will always equal power.
Jesus is my rock, my shield,
his name is a strong tower.
In Him I put my trust, each day I seek His face,
He lets me know He's with me any time and any place.
He gives me divine direction
when I can't see what's ahead.
I'll follow Him because I know
He'll do just what He said.
As long as God is on my side, I will not be defeated.
The enemy has to flee from me.
His plans won't be completed.
I stand on the word of God, that is my foundation.
So I can take authority over a negative situation.
I am my Heavenly Father's child –
clear on my identity –
and wherever I go

I'm determined to show someone
the Christ in me.
I am on the path with purpose and on His path I'll stay.
I am equipped and I'm empowered
for the path He set today.

Positive Point Of Power
Prepared For The Path

When I know that my God has spoken and I am being guided by Him, it creates a confidence in me that allows me to bend and not break. I am anointed for the assignment, steadfast and unmovable, equipped and empowered, and my destiny has been decided. With all that in my favor, above anything I could ask or think, I am never alone!

REFOCUS

It only takes a minute
to say something that is kind.
It doesn't take forever to be nice.
In one split second, you can give a warm hello
or perhaps a little smile will suffice.
It takes the same amount of time
to be discouraging
to someone who has just been mean to you,
as it takes to say a prayer that God would bless them.
Isn't that what we've been called to do?
To say a word of thanks for what you have right now.
A quick gesture of real, heartfelt gratitude
may not change your present situation,
but while you're in it,
it will change your attitude
The time that's spent in grumbling or complaining
about things over which we've no control
is better spent in praise and adoration
for an awesome God whose loving hand we hold.
There's time to make a difference in someone else,
time to be a blessing, great or small;
time to worship, time to praise the loving God
who fashioned everything and knows it all.
So as you go about your day today,
you may just want to shift a thing or two
and take time for the things that matter most to God.
After all, that's what we're really here to do.

Positive Point Of Power
Assess, Align, Act Accordingly

Too often thoughts of being a blessing are centered around material, temporal things that will not last. My desire is to be about my Father's business and display the character of Christ in a way that those who encounter me will want to get to know Him. Self-examination will keep me focused on the things that really matter. The right mindset plants the kind of seed that yields a harvest worth more than anything money can buy.

SELF EXAMINATION

Do I really put God first?
Is He always on my mind?
Do I meditate on Him
or think that's wasting too much time?
Is my day filled selfishly
with all the things I have to do
Without inquiring,
"Lord, what would You have me do for You?"
Do I declare,
"He's Lord of all, whatever comes my way."
Is this how I really feel or empty words I say?
Do my actions contradict
that I'm in fact His child?
Do I conduct myself in ways
I know will make the Father smile?
Am I one way in His presence,
another with a friend
that may lead me to be tempted
and then fall into sin?
Father, please forgive me
if I haven't done my part.
Let me seek You with clean hands
and come with a pure heart.
Let my time in worship
be first order of the day.
Let me be relentless
as I do Your will Your way.

Positive Point Of Power
Today I Examine Myself

It is necessary to periodically examine myself to ensure I am the example of love, gratitude, peace, and power that will make God smile. I need to inquire within myself and be honest in the response as to who I am in Him. I am staying on the potter's wheel allowing God to continue molding me and shaping me so that my actions will never contradict my testimony.

STANDING
IN THE GAP

Father, thank You for the time
You give each of us,
for every wonderful day.
We are grateful to be alive to do Your work
and do Your will Your way
We have a special request of You, Lord
because we know of Your awesome power.
We know how much You love us
and You show us hour by hour.
But today we want You to answer a prayer
in a way no one can deny.
Today we stand for someone else
who has become too weary to try.
Someone feels they've done all they can,
they don't know what else to do.
We know that because You are sovereign God,
it's a perfect opportunity for you.
Their hope seems to be fading, their faith is failing too.
They're tired in their body;
Father, do what only You can do.
Doubt and discouragement are attempting
to make their move again
but your child still has just enough strength
to call upon Your name.
Hear their cry today.
Oh Lord, dispatch angels to help them stand.
Move on their behalf, give them favor for your plan.

Keep a high hedge of protection 'round them
as You show them grace.
Show them mercy, Father,
for only You can fill that empty place.
Divinely intervene on their behalf
with supernatural provision.
Father as they seek Your face,
be sure to give them wisdom.
Their requests seem to be so big to them,
but we know what You can do.
We press in prayer and stand in the gap
sending these requests to You.
Be God for someone who needs You right now.
Lord, we give You the honor You're due.
Remember, as you're praying for somebody else,
someone is praying for you.

Positive Point Of Power
I Am Someone's Warrior

When I think of lessons learned, understanding that
everything is not about me, has been an invaluable key.
Through prayer it will unlock blessings for someone who
needs to know that You, Father God, are real.

TAKE CONTROL

God has given you mercy.
God has given you grace.
He gives you guidance and instructions
so that you can run this race.
He gives you wisdom and discernment.
He gives you power to choose
and that's the greatest weapon
that He's given you to use.
You know before you entered the earth,
God already had a plan.
You know He's always with you.
You're etched in the palm of His hand.
Yet at times when trouble comes
you want to hide and retreat.
Sometimes before the fight begins,
you're already contemplating defeat.
You're more than a conqueror
and if that's what God said,
you know He's already equipped you
for what might lie ahead.
Don't give up, don't cower,
for in you there is power.
Regardless of what you see,
resist the devil and he will flee.
You've been chosen and selected
to expect the unexpected
and you have everything you need.
Lean on God, you will succeed.
Even when you perceive

that trouble might be drawing nigh
there's always a Word in the Word
that you'll be able to apply.
Whatever you are facing, you are not in it alone.
When you seek His face,
you get direction from the throne.
He has given you power and authority,
move with faith and trust in God and in His sovereignty.

Positive Point Of Power
I Will Not Relinquish My Authority

I am governed by the Word of God. I will never compromise who I am and to whom I belong to make someone else comfortable. But I can rise above the noise of life, bring calm to chaos, be determined rather than disappointed, activate my anointing and be the difference that will have a positive impact on the world.

TALKING TO MYSELF

You woke up this morning
knowing you had a lot to do.
But before you go any further,
what have you said to you about you.
You're determined to do for others.
You'll be intentional in your service.
You've prayed for everyone in need
and nothing makes you nervous.
But what have you actually said about you?
What things did you speak?
At times you need to encourage yourself
and speak life to you where you're weak.
Did you say, "The joy of the Lord is my strength?"
Or perhaps, "I'm fearfully and wonderfully made?"
Or maybe, "When I hear the voice of the Lord,
I will trust and obey?"
It may be as simple as "I am chosen."
Or perhaps a reminder like, "I am blessed."
Or, "I have power over my problems."
Or, "With God, I will pass life's tests."
What have you said to you about you?
Make it positive and make it clear.
Speak over yourself with authority
and you will shift your atmosphere.

Positive Point Of Power
I Declare And Decree Over Me

One of my favorite reminders to keep me in triumph is, 'The most important conversation I will ever have is the one I have with myself.' What someone says to me about me, good or bad, will never carry the same weight as what I say about myself. I believe what I speak, and I will alter what I encounter for the Glory of God.

THANK YOU, LORD

Father God, it's my desire
to spend more time with You.
My hunger and thirst can't be ignored
as I'm constantly seeking You.
But sometimes in Your presence,
I don't know what to say.
I guess that's why I'm glad
we can talk more than once a day,
I want to tell you,
thank You for never leaving me alone.
You paid the price through sacrifice,
and I am not my own.
I surrender all to You... all to You I owe,
because of what You've done for me,
I'll never let You go.
You are always with me, whispering in my ear.
As I listen carefully, Your Words remove all fear.
I listen for Your guidance
on what to do, the way I should take
where I can make a difference
just for the gospel's sake.
Thank You for instructions
on the seed that I should sow,
or when to be the water that will help a seed to grow.
Take me step-by-step, dear Lord,
and I'll go where You lead
for You're the answer to my prayers,
the fulfillment of my need.
There's so much ahead of me,

so much that I can do
to help to save a soul
that's lost by pointing them to you.
As I begin another week, I'm filled with gratitude
for I can show the Christ in me just by my attitude.
Thank You for being God alone,
my heart, Oh Lord, please fill.
Continue Lord, to work on me
so that I can do Your will!

Positive Point Of Power
I Receive What I Need In His Presence

When I am in the presence of God, I get everything I need. His voice places me in a posture to hear Him clearly and a calmness overtakes me. I am anxious for nothing because a sovereign God shows His love for me in ways I could never even imagine. I have hope and a future because He will never let me go.

THE LITTLE THINGS

When you woke up this morning,
you had a plan in mind
of what you needed to accomplish
and how you'd spend your time.
Before you even started,
things began to come your way
that were designed to steal your joy
and meant to take your peace away.
Don't panic and start rushing,
take a moment and reflect
on all the precious little things
you'd otherwise forget:
a soft breeze in the morning,
quiet moments at day's end,
A phone call or an email
from a long-time trusted friend.
You gave yourself permission
to take a little time to walk
and found that when you slowed down,
you engaged in positive self-talk.
Favorite flowers, favorite ice cream,
a hug from a small child,
the time you blessed a stranger,
whatever makes you smile,
the beauty in the sunrise,
the colors at sunset,
the contentment found in little things
can keep you from regret.
So when life's coming at you,

new perspectives can be found
by remembering the little things…
just pause and look around.

Positive Point Of Power
Take Time For The Little Things

So many times, we want to do something big for God. We think that the blessings we bestow on someone else have to be monumental in order to represent the mighty God we serve. It is fulfilling to realize that the presence of the Lord is found in the little things we often take for granted. The rays of sunlight piercing through the clouds; the rain and the rainbow; the breeze and the storm; all reminders that God is still God and evident in the earth.

THINGS ARE TURNING AROUND

We always try to be so strong,
well, I'm not ashamed to say
sometimes I need a little extra help
to get through a difficult day.
We don't want to fall apart or let anybody know
that we've got some broken places.
We don't want the wounds to show.
We've all got baggage from the past
and if you don't tell anyone else,
the least that you can do, to be fair to you,
is admit it to yourself.
It's okay, no one is perfect.
We're all in the same boat
from time to time, it seems we're trying our best
just to stay afloat
That's why we have to turn to the Father
and lay the weight at His feet.
He's greater than... He'll help you to stand...
no condemnation, no defeat.
God will give you what you need,
no matter what you have to face—
strength, power, guidance...
He'll even mend that broken place.
He'll send you a reminder in a message, or a song,
or even through morning worship
so that you can remain strong.
Take heart and be encouraged,

don't give up and don't shut down.
A shift is in the atmosphere...
things are about to turn around.

Positive Point Of Power
It's Turning

As long as God is with me, I have hope that difficulties, once discovered, can be made easier to bear. I don't have to carry the weight of it all. I don't have to reach for reasons. I don't have to cower in a corner. God is there to be the burden bearer and when I turn things over to the Master, He can turn it around.

TIME TO CHOOSE

Here's an important assignment
for those who would be wise,
ask God if He would show you,
your places of compromise.
When it comes to God,
it's not one day in and then one day out.
Once you choose the Savior,
you choose ALL things that He's about.
When we make decisions in our flesh,
we allow some things to slip
and little foxes here and there will change us bit by bit.
We think that things can go our way
without consulting God.
Trust me when I tell you,
that's when things get really hard.
Sometimes when God gives us our way
and then things don't work out,
we blame Him saying,
"Okay God, what was that about."
Surrender your agenda and what you want to do.
Seek His face in worship. Seek His will for you.
Some things we may not understand,
everything's not always clear.
God is always speaking to those with ears to hear.
The world says, when it comes to the Word,
you don't have to hear it.
God says not only hear His Word,
but try it by the Spirit.
None of us are perfect, we die to self each day.

But only when you make a choice to do His will His way
will you truly grow in God
and into who He's called you to be.
You must trust him and surrender all to His sovereignty
Let Him show you where you're in error,
then accept correction
and you'll make Godly choices
as you follow His direction.
With God's help, examine yourself,
and Let Him renew you mind.
Then even when you're going through,
you'll still choose God every time.

Positive Point Of Power
I Choose God

As hard as self-examination may seem to be, it is
necessary to show me where I am in error. Perfection is
not expected, mistakes can be accepted, but correction
will keep me on the path – righteous and steadfast –
without wavering.

"Father, You have been so good to me. My desire is to
please You coming to You with clean hands and a pure
heart. You are my everything and I will choose you
every time."

TURN IT OVER

I was thinking when I woke up this morning
how I get confused sometimes
over what issues belong to God
and what issues are mine.
I know I'm not the only one—
when things in life go wrong,
we begin to go into "fix it" mode,
after all, you're wise, you're strong...
Yes, you are more than a conqueror
but every battle isn't yours to fight.
Your responsibility is to love one another –
and to show someone His light.
I can handle this on my own.
At least that's what you might think.
Then after you've made a mess, God steps in
and before you can blink.
He's made the crooked places straight,
given you the answer, worked it out.
You may have been confused at first
but later you reflect on what it was all about.
Don't get so hung up on your next
and forget about your now.
Even when you don't understand,
be obedient anyhow.
You don't have to worry.
You need not be concerned.
Just know that everything has purpose
and lessons to be learned.
This may not be a new revelation

and it may not be deep and profound,
let you be you, let God be God
and some things just might turn around.
and this isn't deep and profound,
let you be you, let God be God
and some things just might turn around.

Positive Point Of Power
Turn It Over

I don't know what makes me think that God needs my help. He can do anything and everything all by Himself. What's more, He wants me to lean on Him, depend on Him, trust in Him, receive from Him, and He will bless me with His best. The last thing I want to do is get in His way.

VICTORY

I started out this morning thinking everything was fine.
I'd been talking to the Father and was having quiet time.
My head was filled with positive thoughts
on things I wanted to do.
But before I knew it,
negative vibes were changing my point of view.
I started this downward spiral. It was happening so fast.
I was thinking of disappointment,
and failures from my past.
Hurt… pain… a sad refrain
about things I couldn't fix.
Wait! Hold on! There's nothing wrong.
It's just the enemy up to his tricks!
He wants me to playback fear and put pain on repeat.
He wants me to abort my dreams and give up in defeat.
Notice: the devil is a liar. He might desire my demise.
But it won't work
because I choose to see things through God's eye.
I am blessed. I'm highly favored.
God is with me so, 'I can.'
I will not be defeated. I know who and whose I am.
If the enemy comes at you,
don't be fooled by his evil plot.
He wants you to think you're powerless,
but if you belong to God, you're not.
I began to give God praise
and continued on my way.
Trusting in the God I serve,
'cause the devil lost today!

Positive Point Of Power
Victory Is Mine

I am not ignorant of the devices of the enemy. I give him no airtime and He has no authority over anything concerning me. Greater is He that is in me, and God has given me power over everything that's not like Him. I will give no place or space to what God has defeated and put under my feet. Oh yes, victory is mine!

WAIT

When time seems to be standing still
and no matter what I try,
I feel as if I'm on the sidelines
while life goes speeding by.
That's when I get ahead of God,
moving faster than I should
forgetting when things don't go my way,
they're still working for my good.
If I would stop and seek His face
to find out what to do,
I'd save myself some time and trouble
and not have to go through
some struggles or some trials.
But God is teaching me.
He's molding me, He's shaping me
so that I can be
who and what He had in mind
when He placed me in the earth.
From my parents to my purpose,
He planned it all before my birth.
I have to keep myself in check.
Turn my thoughts to Him each day.
His plans for me are pre-arranged
and at times I'm in His way.

Thank You for the reminder,
Lord. I know what I must do
when things seem to be standing still,
I must rest in you.

I won't begin to question,
worry, compare, complain, or fret.
Instead, I'll praise and worship You,
knowing You're not through with me yet.
Your promises will come to pass and until they do,
I'll be of good courage, waiting patiently on You.

Positive Point Of Power
Check Yourself

I am not just moving according to God's plans, purpose, and agenda, I am operating by His timetable. I am in constant communication with my Heavenly Father so that I can keep myself in sync with His rhythm as He orchestrates all things concerning me.

Life is so much better when I wait on the Lord.

WISE COUNSEL

Are you in a struggle? Facing some tests or trials?
Getting a little weary? Tired of delays
that feel like denials?
When things don't come together
the way we think they should,
the Bible says all things will work together
for the good of those who love the Lord...
the called according to His purpose.
There's no need to be afraid,
nothing should make you nervous.
You're leaning on the Rock.
He's your buckler. He's your shield.
Just wait on the Lord.
In time, His plan will be revealed.
And even if it isn't, if you never know the why,
There's still no need to pout and doubt,
or moan and groan, or cry.
God is forever faithful.
Think of all He's brought you through
in the eleventh hour when you didn't know what to do.
And now you face a challenge,
and you want to cut and run,
or quit, throwing your hands up saying,
"You know what, I'm done."
Sorry, there's no time for that.
Rise and get back in the race.
Since God is always with you,
there's nothing you can't face.
Superimpose the Word over every situation.

Knowing you're a conqueror
should be your motivation
to keep moving, to keep striving,
to keep pressing, stay on track.
You've already got the victory
so why would you turn back?
Stay encouraged. Trust the Lord.
Believe His Word and pray.
You may still face a battle,
but You won the fight today!

Positive Point Of Power
In The End, I Win

When I need to encourage myself, when I find myself getting tired or discouraged...

I know where my help comes from...
I know how to be uplifted...
I know the way to get directions...
I know my strength can be renewed...

The Word of the Lord gives me whatever I need to rise above the noise of life and never, ever give up! I know the outcome, the end of the story, what happens when it's all said and done, and I am in place for the win.

YES, LORD... YES!

You call Him, Abba Father.
You say that you are His.
If that's a fact, to stay on track, take this little quiz.
When you pass someone today,
will they see the Christ in you?
Do you think that He is evident
in what you say and do?
In your daily conversation,
will they hear His Words come through?
Will you be an example
that His promises are true?
Will you work in excellence
as unto the Lord?
Can you be a peacemaker and be on one accord
even when you disagree?
If God says you should,
will you put yourself aside for the greater good?
Do you give thanks
IN all things and when things go wrong,
will you be found still praising,
singing God a worship song?
How'd you do? Score 100?
or did you just do okay?
You see, you'll face some type of test,
each and every day.
How prepared will you be to take the next exam?
How equipped are you to represent the great 'I Am?'
You may have to study more, and some things reassess,
but next time you're asked, if you passed,

your answer will be "YES!"

Positive Point Of Power
I'm Prepared To Pass

God is not looking for the proficient, He's looking for the available. He will place in you whatever you need to be equipped and empowered to be used for His glory and His plans to bring the Kingdom into the earth. He wants someone who will say yes to His will, and His way and tell somebody the good news that Jesus is alive! I say, yes, Lord, yes!!

ABOUT THE AUTHOR

Andrea L. Hines
*Mother, Grandmother, Author, Poet, Speaker,
Entrepreneur, Doctor of Divinity, Certified Life Coach
and Radio Host*

This lady of many talents is a native of Washington, D.C. who now resides in Raleigh, NC. She often says that moving to the "quiet beauty of the Carolinas" deepened her relationship with God and caused her creativity to flow freely.

Andrea has over thirty years of experience in the performing arts as an actor, playwright and director, with performances in numerous community theater and film projects. She has been a narrator for the North Carolina Library for the Blind and Physically Handicapped; and continues to enjoy lending her voice to any number of voice-over projects.

Her poetic work has been featured in local newspapers, on Blue Mountain Arts greeting cards and products, and included in numerous anthologies. She has written a collection of inspirational verses titled 'When He Whispers', words of encouragement inspired by her granddaughter titled, 'Nanny Nuggets'; and inspiration through affirmations – When Life Speaks, You Speak Life. While Andrea has authored story poems, greeting cards and other works, she says God has given her the ability to write the words people often think but can't express.

She introduced her company, A's Accents in 1994. Her performance and product showcase, "...A Work in Progress.," weaves a story of life experiences through her original verses with musical interludes. "A Reading for His Glory" provides a more intimate atmosphere with smaller groups, giving them the opportunity to interact with the author on a more personal level. Her style and ability to uplift the heart has made her a favorite speaker in areas from commencement exercises to conferences. You can see her on her You Tube channel – Andrea L. Hines – and hear her as she hosts programs on her own internet radio/TV station, ALH Broadcasting, an affiliate of SIBN – Streaming Inspirational Broadcast Network.

Andrea has received an honorary Doctorate Degree of Divinity and also serves as an Elder at The River Church in Durham, NC. She is a Certified Life Coach, and owner of C.L.A.S.S Coaching and Consulting-Cultivating Lives and Success Strategies. She believes God has blessed her with certain gifts, and only hopes that whatever she creates will be to His glory and a blessing to someone else.

www.ingramcontent.com/pod-product-compliance
Lightning Source LLC
Chambersburg PA
CBHW031225120626
46545CB00003B/989